The Daily Telegraph

THE BEST OF

1999

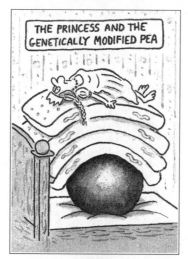

ORION

Orion Books
A division of the Orion Publishing Group Ltd
Orion House
5 Upper St Martin's Lane
London WC2H 9EA

First published by Orion Books in 1999

The right of Matthew Pritchett to be identified as the
author of this work has been asserted by him in accordance
with the Copyright, Designs and Patents Act, 1988

A CIP catalogue record for this book
is available from the British Library

ISBN 0 75282 706 5

Printed and bound in Great Britain by
The Guernsey Press Co. Ltd, Guernsey, C. I.

THE BEST OF

'There's talk of redundancies'

Weather or not

Television

'Coming up, a woman confesses to her horrified husband, I Hosted a Daytime TV Show'

'Wow, there are even 50 channels showing only programmes on proportional representation'

Lords Reform

'Isn't it time you
were abolished, dear?'

'Believe me, if you'd met
my son you'd be against
hereditary peerages'

Lords Reform

'Their numbers have to be controlled and this is the most humane way'

Europe

'Would you get the report on nepotism from my mummy's office, please'

'I'm afraid he's resigned for a couple of hours — he should be back after lunch'

EC Commission forced to resign . . .

Europe

'Does the Eurostar to Brussels connect with the EU Gravy Train?'

'No, my husband is counting the European election votes — he'll be back any minute'

. . . and the voter couldn't care less

Devolution Apathy

Fear of Flying

'...And remember, break when I say break, and no punching below the belt'

Clinton's Impeachment

The whole world watches . . .

Clinton's Impeachment

'Remind me, is our relationship with America special or inappropriate?'

Clinton's Impeachment

'I dreamt Kenneth Starr wrote
a detailed report on my
sex life and it didn't even
fill half a sheet of paper'

'Apparently the average
male thinks about Clinton's
impeachment every 22 seconds'

Clinton's Impeachment

'My goodness, now even Buddy is making a scathing attack on Clinton'

'Shoot anyone who arrives with a Valentine card for President Clinton'

A Sporting Life

Wet Wimbledon

A Sporting Life

A Sporting Life

'I happen to believe, if you've
got the young boy Owen up
front with Shearer, you need
Gascoigne to deliver the ball
into the box . . .'

'Is this for something
I did in a previous life?'

Hoddle: England coach / spiritual leader

A Sporting Life

Everyone loves
Manchester United . . .

. . . but Murdoch fails
to buy them

Sports Scandal

'If I give you £10 will you go and discuss the Olympic bribes scandal somewhere else?'

TOUR DE FRANCE ROW

'Ah, vicar, I couldn't help noticing you got from the church to the rectory in a suspiciously short time'

Money Matters

'Darling, come out here
and watch the Euro
slowly going down'

'This is our best trader –
he can smell fear'

Money Matters

'Dad won't let me have a yoyo.
He's a stockbroker and it
reminds him too much of work'

'Remember the value of your
shares can go further down as
well as right down'

Money Matters

'It seems an awful lot of fuss over a 0.5% cut in interest rates'

'. . . . . . I might rally'

A Question of Politics

Labour tries to control its MPs . . .

A Question of Politics

. . . and everyone else . . .

A Question of Politics

'Sometimes you can
hear a distant boom as
Jack Cunningham goes
through the expenses barrier'

. . . as they acquire a taste for the high life

A Question of Politics

'I know I'll be accused of being a bigot but I find there's something distasteful about Lib-Lab partnerships'

'It's amazing, I've already forgotten where I was when I heard the news'

A Question of Politics

Former Tory minister
Jonathan Aitken sent
to prison . . .

. . . and takes up poetry

Politics: The Budget

'I think I preferred the
Budget before I understood it'

'My accountant says we
should get drunk and
start a family'

The Nanny State

'Waiter, the fly in my soup would like to read the new food safety proposals'

'Darling, we're going to hear the gentle patter of government advice booklets coming through the letter box'

Passport Crisis

'. . . And here's another one
of us in the queue at the
passport office'

'I'm taking a year off
before university to try
to get a passport'

The Health Service

The Health Service

The Health Service

'Should anything happen to me, I want a hospital to have my bed'

'Don't have a heart attack or the neighbours will think we're lower class'

The Health Service

'I'd like a racist to be given my ingrowing toenail'

Racist conditions . . .

. . . and a change in donor regulations

Cloning

'Same again?'

Cloning

The Royals

Charles doesn't propose . . .

. . . and Edward finally does

The Royals

The Sun nearly spoils the day

The Royals

'No saucers, I'm cutting down on the pomp and ceremony'

MONA LISA

'It's been digitally enhanced'

Less splendour . . .

. . . but computer-enhanced smiles

The Police

The Police

'Come out slowly and tell us you think the police are doing a great job'

'In the old days we'd just get a clip round the ear'

The Police

'You only stopped me
because I'm green'

'It's infuriating – every time
I go out I'm stopped by
police recruitment officers'

GM Food

'I just want to say thank you'

'That's not beef-on-the-bone, it's a genetically modified tomato'

GM Food

'We've developed a soya bean that is against a single currency, but is pro-Europe'

GM Food

'The trouble is, you don't know what you're pollinating these days'

'Excuse me, is that fruit genetically modified?'

More Food Scares

Farming in Crisis . . .

'I've become a vegetarian – I can't bear the cruel way some supermarkets treat farmers'

Mary had a little lamb
Its fleece was white as snow
She had to shoot it through
 the head
The lamb price fell so low

Farming in Crisis . . .

'I have several bank accounts and I use a system of overdraft rotation'

. . . But Beef Ban Finally Lifted

'The good news is we can go to Europe, the bad news is the Blairs have got the Tuscan villa we wanted'

Balkans Conflict

'We've seriously degraded his dinner party capabilities'

'There goes the neighbourhood'

NATO hits Milosevic . . .

Balkans Conflict

'Either Nato has dropped a graphite bomb in our bathroom or the bulb has gone again'

. . . sometimes . . .

Balkans Conflict

'I tried to get to the shops but
cloud cover prevented me
from reaching my target'

'Look out! Clouds
at seven o'clock!'

. . . weather permitting

Balkans Conflict

'Unless I get positive proof that they are starting to leave I'm going to begin bombing them'

Pinochet

'General Pinochet has escaped!'

Thatcher's for . . .

'Now you might feel a slight twinge when I do this'

. . . Government against

Pinochet

'It would help us enormously, General Pinochet, if you claimed you were a member of the IRA'

'I'd like you to be disqualified from presiding over this case, M'lud, because of your close links with the legal profession'

The legal wranglings continue

Spies R Us

'I've just discovered you're NOT an MI6 agent and you haven't been on a top secret mission'

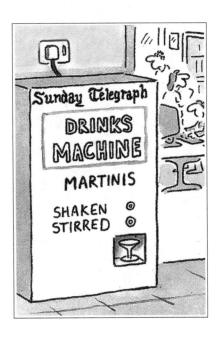

They're everywhere

Transport Traumas

'You can set your watch by these trains – if that's the 7.30 it must be lunchtime'

Transport Traumas

Diesel Tax protest

Transport Traumas

Turbulence in the
boardroom . . .

. . . and in the air

Transport Traumas

Anti-smoking

'There, now I can't even
find my cigarettes'

'It will all be worthwhile if it
stops just one young person
going into advertising'

End of the World?

Artistic Licence

'One ticket to see Monet's Waterlilies, please'

Drugs

'How much cocaine can I get
for 250 milk bottle tops?'

From children's TV . . .

. . . to the aristocracy

And finally . . .

'They're not sapphires,
they're Viagra pills'

And finally . . .

'It's not really, but I'm hoping
Greenpeace will break in
and mow it'

And finally . . .

"*We call it 'Couple Waiting for a Jubilee Line Train'*"

And finally . . .

'That sounds a bad idea . . .'

'HELLO! I got your name
and address from an
MI6 list on the internet'

And finally . . .

'Ridiculous! My six-year-old son could have done that!'

And finally . . .

'The staff have been impossible
since Tony Blair told them
they're middle class'

And finally . . .

'I bought it because
Delia Smith has one'

And finally . . .

'Britons illiterate! Get a friend to read all about it!'

'There isn't time to dial their new phone number – I'll write them a letter instead'

And finally . . .

'On a clear day you can see
our car for £3,000 less
than we paid for it'

And finally . . .

'Hello, darling, I've done most of the shopping, but did you say washing powder was cheaper in Spain or France?'

And finally . . .

'If we don't want our child to visit the Millennium Dome when should we try to conceive?'

'I've worked out that if Bill Gates followed your racing tips he'd be bankrupt by 2005'

And finally . . .